PARKS & MONUMENTS OF CALIFORNIA

A Scenic Guide

National Park Service — YOSEMITE'S EL CAPITAN

A RENAISSANCE HOUSE PUBLICATION

© Copyright 1992 by Eleanor H. Ayer. Printed in the United States of America. All rights reserved. This book or any parts thereof, may not be reproduced in any manner whatsoever without written permission of the publisher:

ISBN: 1-55838-119-8

RENAISSANCE HOUSE
A Division of Jende-Hagan, Inc.
541 Oak Street ~ P.O. Box 177
Frederick, CO 80530

Cover Photo of Rainbow Falls, courtesy Wymond Eckhardt, Devils Postpile National Monument

10 9 8 7 6 5 4 3 2 1

Welcome

We were well into preparation of this guide before we began to feel guilty. Our purpose in publishing it was to promote the exquisite beauty of California's national parklands and encourage travelers to visit them. But by doing this, we seemed to be contributing to a growing problem: that of America's parks being loved to death. In sheer numbers, American travelers are putting a strain on park resources and threatening the isolation of the wilderness they cherish.

The solution is not to stay at home. These parks and cultural heritage centers were set aside to be appreciated by the American public. The parks encourage travelers to visit--but in a responsible, conservation-minded manner. If our national parklands are to remain accessible to us, we must take personal responsibility for their protection and sacredness.

With that in mind, we reassessed our approach to this book. We contacted the parks, telling them that we planned to make this an ecological, environmentally sensitive guide. We asked them to offer tips on how to protect natural and cultural resources at their areas. Most were very appreciative, and indicated that this approach was much needed.

Throughout the text are many suggestions for making an environmental conscionable visit to the parks. Within the articles you will find information on endangered plants or animals, ideas on how to interact with wildlife, advice on where you should or shouldn't walk, hike, bike, or drive. But one idea must be stressed above all: *Use common sense and good ethics.* That's all it really takes.

California also has a rich endowment of state parks and state beaches. Those areas are administered by a different agency than the national parklands and they will be explored in a future volume of **The California Traveler** series. But the #1 visitation rule remains the same: treat the property like your own--because it is!

As you plan your scenic tour of the Golden State, take along some of these other fine guidebooks in **The California Traveler** series:

Whale Watching and Marine Life
California Missions
California's Wine Country
Railroads of California

A Thank-You to Greg Gnesios at the Whiskeytown Unit and to the Interpretive Specialists at each of the park areas for their reading of the text prior to publication. They have insured the accuracy of this ***California Traveler*** *guide.*

National Park Service   POINT REYES NATIONAL SEASHORE

CONTENTS

Cabrillo National Monument	4
Joshua Tree National Monument	7
Santa Monica Mountains N.R.A.	9
Channel Islands National Park	11
Death Valley National Monument	14
Sequoia & Kings Canyon National Park	17
Devils Postpile	20
Yosemite National Park	22
Pinnacles National Monument	28
Eugene O'Neill N.H.S.	29
Muir Woods National Monument	30
John Muir National Historic Site	32
Golden Gate N.R.A.	33
Point Reyes National Seashore	35
Lassen Volcanic National Park	38
Lava Beds National Monument	40
Whiskeytown-Shasta-Trinity N.R.A.	42
Redwood National Park	44
Our Endangered Parks	46
Names & Numbers	48

Cabrillo Nat. Mon.   STATUE TO THE CONQUISTADOR

CABRILLO NATIONAL MONUMENT

The man for whom this national monument is named is credited with the discovery of California. Looking for gold (as well as a little glory), Cabrillo sailed into what is now San Diego Bay on September 28, 1542, setting foot in a land then inhabited by people who greeted him wearing animal skins. Cabrillo continued up the coast to today's San Miguel. There, he met with disaster while trying to break up a fight between his men and the native Indians. A leg broken during a November scuffle became infected with gangrene, and six weeks later Juan Rodriguez Cabrillo was dead.

A statue of the conquistador stands today on a hilltop at the southern tip of Point Loma in the city of San Diego. Since 1913, this land has been preserved as a national monument. In addition to its beautiful view of the city, bay, and ocean, there are many reasons why Cabrillo makes a good destination for travelers.

One reason is the gray whale migration. Every year, from late December to late February, this great natural phenomenon takes place just offshore from Cabrillo. Thousands of gray whales head south from the Arctic Ocean, traveling 5,000 miles to the warmer waters of Baja, where pregnant females give birth to their young and care for them until they are old enough to make

San Diego Natural History Museum   SUCCESSFUL WHALE WATCHING

the trip home in March or April. In their migration, the whales come close enough to Point Loma that they can be seen easily from the monument grounds. Here an overlook area and visitor center have been established to answer travelers' questions about these massive mammals. Spouts in the ocean beyond the kelp beds identify good spots to view grays.

For those wishing a closer look, a number of companies offer whale watching cruises. Grays sometimes come close enough to small boats that people can touch them, but this is dangerous both for the whale and the passengers.

During the early and mid-19th century, when whaling was big business, grays were hunted nearly to extinction. Since 1946, the California grays have been protected, which has greatly increased their numbers. But they are still in danger from polluted waters and human encroachment on their environment. Strict regulations apply to whale watching cruisers, such as not separating a cow from her calf and not herding whales into a group. Nevertheless, if we are to preserve this fantastic animal, individual travelers must use good judgment when interacting with the grays or their environment.

Another marine attraction at Cabrillo is the tidepools just off the west shore of Point Loma. Here among the rocks and the surf live dozens of unique marine plants and animals such as dead man's fingers and flowery anemones. Travelers wishing to go

Cabrillo National Monument   OLD POINT LOMA LIGHTHOUSE

tidepooling should plan a visit during low tide, preferably not in the summer. Rangers at the monument can suggest best times and places.

A major point of historical interest at Cabrillo is the Old Point Loma Lighthouse. Built in 1855, when the California Gold Rush and resultant settlement caused an increase in sea traffic in the San Diego area, the Point Loma light remained operational until 1891. During its glory days, it was the highest navigational beacon in America. But therein lay a problem and the reason for its closing. Because the tower rose 462 feet high, low level clouds would often settle below it, obstructing sailors' view of the light. So it was that a new lighthouse was built at a lower elevation which has operated continuously since 1891.

Today Old Point Loma serves as a museum of west coast lighthouse keeping during the 1880s. Visitors can see how a lighthouse keeper and his family lived and try to imagine how he got by on the $1000 annual salary. Apparently many did not, for the Point Loma Light went through 22 assistant keepers in 36 years!

Travelers to Cabrillo can take a two-mile round trip hike along Bayside Trail from the lighthouse through the coastal chaparral life zone. Hikers are asked not to collect or remove natural objects, to stay on marked walkways, to conserve water while at the monument, and to reduce traffic by walking or bicycling into the park whenever possible.

National Park Service, Richard Frear JOSHUA TREE NAT. MON.

JOSHUA TREE NAT. MON.

The plant from which this national monument takes its name is a large yucca belonging to the agave family. The Joshua tree was named by early Mormon settlers who thought its misshapen form looked like Joshua beckoning them farther west. These vegetative sentinels abound in the Mohave Desert at elevations above 3,000 feet, particularly in the central and western sections of the monument. Here, Joshua trees reach heights of 20 to 30 feet.

Joshua Tree National Monument is located just east of Palm Springs, north of I-10. Here, on an average summer day, temperatures range from 100-110 degrees. Rainfall is sparse, 4 to 8 inches a year, depending on elevation. The monument is made up of two deserts. Below 3,000 feet, in the eastern half, is the Colorado Desert, where the characteristic plant is the creosote bush. In the western portion is the Mohave Desert, which is generally higher and wetter.

Scattered amid this arid land are five oases, the few areas of the desert where water can be found at or near the surface. These watering areas are known to the many forms of wildlife that inhabit the monument, from coyotes and jackrabbits to less familiar creatures such as sidewinders, golden eagles, tarantulas, and stinkbugs. Rattlesnakes are common here, but environmentally aware travelers should know that these reptiles are much afraid of man. If not bothered by trespassers to their land, they will keep to themselves.

One animal at the monument which requires special consideration is the desert tortoise. With its distinctive high-domed shell and elephant-like limbs, this creature is a threatened species. Although it may be encouraged on its way across the road, travelers are asked not to touch or move the animal. Pets must be kept within 100 yards of roads or campgrounds. The scent of a dog can scare wildlife away from a much-needed watering hole for days--which is often too long in this arid environment.

Joshua Tree offers excellent hiking and camping opportunities. But entering this delicate ecosystem requires travelers to accept responsibility for its care. Five species of plants at the monument are currently endangered or threatened, but we must treat all with equal care. The desert is a very fragile environment. A wildflower trampled by a hiking boot or a jumping cholla crushed by a mountain bike can take years, if ever, to regenerate.

Within the monument there are 3500 established rock climbs, making it one of the most popular climbing areas in the world. Trash, soil erosion and compaction, damage to vegetation, disposal of human waste, damage to cultural resources, and general overcrowding have become grave concerns to park managers. Hidden Valley is one climbing area which suffers greatly from overuse. To address these concerns, Joshua Tree distributes a brochure called "Important Climber Information" which every concerned traveler should request.

Because it is a national monument, all natural and cultural resources at Joshua Tree are protected and may not be removed. This includes artifacts and remnants from the Lost Horse, Desert Queen, and Desert Ranch gold mines which were prospected during the late 1800s and early 1900s. These mine shafts are unstable and dangerous and should not be entered.

In times long before the prospectors, Pinto Man hunted along the banks of a now dry river in the monument. Other prehistoric people left primitive art work on rock walls. Rock climbing within 50 feet of this art work is today prohibited, in an effort to protect it from skin oils, chalk marks, and boot soles. Later Indians produced pottery, projectile points, stone tools and other artifacts. Their remnants must not be disturbed by those of us visiting the monument today.

National Park Service — SATWIWA SITE, RANCHO SIERRA VISTA

SANTA MONICA MTS. NRA

Los Angeles' vast (150,000 acre) playground just north of the city offers a delightful variety of parks which include beaches, mountains, lagoons, canyons, ranches, and other areas of natural and cultural interest. Travelers to this national recreation area can hike, picnic, take in a concert, go surfing, visit a movie set, or participate in any of dozens of activities offered at the various sites each day.

The Santa Monica Mountains are somewhat unique in being an east-west range. Rising from Griffith Park in the center of the city, they project southward toward Santa Monica Bay and west to Point Mugu, their high peaks facing the ocean. The many sites, from ranches to state parks, to beaches, cover a 50-mile stretch from east to west.

In 1978, after 15 years of effort, this land was set aside for the burgeoning number of residents and visitors to this area. Unlike many federal areas, this NRA is not managed by one body. Federal, state, county, community, and private interests work cooperatively to administer the many different segments.

Twenty beach areas run along 47 miles of coastline from Point Mugu south to the City of Santa Monica. Depending on the site, travelers can enjoy the solitude of a tidepool or lie elbow-to-elbow with fellow sun-worshippers on a public beach. Some beaches offer hiking trails, and fishing holes. At others, travelers can bicycle, surf, swim or picnic.

National Park Service   SITE OF RESTORED WESTERN MOVIE SET

Visitors to the mountain area can ride horses, go mountain biking, hike, or take in cultural exhibits. The Getty Museum, housing paintings and sculptures from the collection of J. Paul Getty, is one of the areas within the NRA. At Will Rogers State Historic Park, there are tours of the Rogers' home, as well as weekend polo matches, and hiking along the Backbone Trail. Ultimately this trail will extend 55 miles through the NRA, connecting each of its major parklands.

The Santa Monica Mountains region is home to the unique coastal mediterranean ecosystem, found in only a few places worldwide. At the Circle X Ranch Site are stands of red shanks chaparral, indigenous only from Palm Springs to Baja. The riparian community, another important ecosystem, is found in canyon bottoms near permanent water. Happy Hollow Camp, also in the Circle X Ranch Site is a good example.

What is today the Santa Monica Mountains NRA was once home to the Chumash Indians. Rancho Sierra Vista, one of the parkland areas, is thought to have been a Chumash trade/travel route. The Satwiwa Site within this area is now a cultural center for descendants of the Chumash as well as the Gabrielino and other native peoples. A Chumash village once located here was called Satwiwa, meaning "the bluffs."

The environmentally considerate traveler must be very careful of fire in the Santa Monica parklands. Although natural fires play an important role in recycling nutrients through the chaparral ecosystem, man-caused fires threaten to destroy it. Campfire coals can become raging infernos when fanned by high winds called Santa Anas, common to this region. Therefore, open fires are prohibited and smoking is not allowed on the trails.

National Park Service AN AERIAL VIEW OF SANTA BARBARA ISLAND

CHANNEL ISLANDS NAT. PARK

A dozen miles offshore from Point Mugu in the Santa Monica Mountains NRA lies a chain of islands, five of which comprise Channel Islands National Park. Regular boat service to the five islands is available through the park concessionaire from the visitor center on the mainland. Here also is an exhibit area featuring Chumash Indian artifacts, an indoor tidepool, and a simulated caliche ghost forest.

Travelers to the islands will come first to Anacapa, located 11 miles southwest of Oxnard. This 1-sq. mi. island is comprised of three smaller islands: East, Middle, and West Anacapa. The western slopes are home to the endangered brown pelican, which can be spotted here at any time of the year. This islet has been named a Research Natural Area, closed to public use, in an effort to protect the pelican rookery. But off its southeast corner, in an area called Frenchy's Cove, is a beach and snorkeling area. Many tidepools are here, offering an amazing selection of marine wildlife for the traveler to view. But these tidepools are protected, which means nothing may be taken.

The trademark of the Channel Islands is a natural bridge called Arch Rock on Anacapa. This 40-foot high arch is at the east end of the island. Also on East Anacapa is a lighthouse to keep sailors away from the island's rocky shores. Before its transition to automatic lighting in 1966, the lighthouse had a keeper who lived on the island.

Elsewhere on Anacapa are scuba and skin diving areas. Off the middle islet is the wreck of the steamer *Winfield Scott* which sank in 1853. The submerged remains may be photographed, but not removed from the wreckage area.

Next comes the chain's largest island, Santa Cruz, 96 sq. mi. of steep cliffs, gigantic sea caves, sandy beaches, and coves. More than 600 plant species--nine of them occurring only on Santa Cruz--and 140 species of land birds live here. Santa Cruz also claims the highest point in the island chain: 2,400 feet.

On this island, the Chumash Indians lived for more than 6,000 years. Juan Rodriguez Cabrillo, the explorer credited with discovering California, probably encountered more than 2,000 of the natives when he reached the island in 1542. In the mid-19th century, a Mexican land grant led to ranching operations here, but in recent years the island has been under private ownership. Travelers may not land on Santa Cruz unless they are on an authorized trip, such as those conducted by The Nature Conservancy.

Continuing west in the chain, travelers come to Santa Rosa, second largest of the islands. A permit is required to land here or travelers may fly in. Grasslands cover about 85 percent of Santa Rosa, but it also contains high mountains, canyons, volcanic formations and fossil beds. On the rocky terraces are large groups of black abalone, and the coastal waters are home to harbor seals. Interesting land animals include the spotted skunk, the island fox, and the gopher snake. Surrounding the entire island are huge beds of kelp, making this a wonderful natural nursery for young marine life. Native Cumash Indians most certainly lived on Santa Rosa, as well as later-day Spanish cattle ranchers.

Santa Rosa may contain the grave of explorer Juan Rodriguez Cabrillo, although it is not certain that he is buried here. Cabrillo is, however, thought to have wintered and died at Cuyler Harbor on San Miguel, westernmost of the Channel Islands, in 1543. A monument to him was erected here in 1937. In the 1940s and '50s, San Miguel was used as a bombing range, and live ammunition can still be found in the shifting sands. Some 500 archaeological sites, many of them undisturbed, dot the island.

San Miguel is famous for its caliche, the calcium carbonate deposits that form on rocks. The caliche "forest" in the center of the island is an intriguing collection of these mineral sand castings, but travelers must leave the caliche intact and untouched. Among the natural inhabitants of San Miguel are sea lions,

National Park Service A CHANNEL ISLAND SEAL

island foxes, and seals. Coreopsis--the sunflower that can reach heights of ten feet--and other flowering plants put on beautiful displays of color in springtime.

Approximately 40 miles south of Anacapa is the fifth island in the park, Santa Barbara, named by explorer Vizcaino who landed here on Saint Barbara's Day in 1602. A lack of fresh water kept native Indians away from the island, but by 1920, settlers were farming and grazing here, to the detriment of the native vegetation. California sea lions and elephant seals breed on Santa Barbara, and the threatened island night lizard lives here as well. The island offers more than five miles of hiking, but travelers should pack a hat and plenty of water, as there are no shade trees.

Protection of natural and cultural resources is a major concern on these harsh but dynamically beautifully islands. Travelers should keep in mind these rules of good common sense:

* Pack out all trash.
* Do not harass marine mammals such as seals, whales, and sea lions.
* Collect nothing out of tidepools.
* Do not disturb native plant life, such as the coreopsis.

Many of the tidepools are now nearly void of marine life due to overuse by humans over several decades. Let's not contribute to the problem.

Death Valley Nat. Mon.

Welcome to the lowest and hottest place in North America. On an *average* July day in Death Valley, look for temperatures of 116 degrees F. In fact, from May through September, daytime temperatures average more than 100 degrees. Desert rainfall during these months is just what you might expect: an average *total* of 1/3 of an inch. The entire annual rainfall in Death Valley is just 1.65 inches.

This unique and amazing California desert houses Badwater, America's lowest geographic point, located 282 feet below sea level. But it is also home to 11,049-foot Telescope Peak. The altitude difference between these locations is more than two miles, one of the greatest vertical rises in the United States. This drastic change is the result of geologic faulting within the monument; the valley was formed when the central portion dropped and the mountains thrust up.

This national monument is 1-1/2 times as large as the entire state of Delaware, and its geology offers a nearly complete record of Earth's history. The rocks represent all of the eras and most of the periods of geologic time. It can be confusing, however, for the novice to track, for the rock record has been rearranged by erosion. Although it doesn't rain often at Death Valley, when it does, the water washes down the canyons, carrying bits and pieces of rock and sand from the different periods down to the valley floor and piling them there for some determined geologist to figure out.

The climate in Death Valley is unforgiving, yet some 900 species of plants live here; for 20 of those types, Death Valley is their only home. These desert plants have adapted to their environment by a variety of ingenious means. Some can exist on water with a salt content of up to 5%; others have evolved special protective coverings to cut down on water loss. Still others shed their leaves during the driest months.

A wide selection of wildlife also makes its home in Death Valley. Here live more than 230 kinds of birds, 17 kinds of lizards and 19 kinds of snakes. As would seem sensible, most desert creatures are nocturnal. The mountain areas of Death Valley support some of the larger wildlife, such as bighorn sheep.

There have been human inhabitants at the monument since 6000 B.C. When the earliest people lived here, 90-mile-long Lake Manley covered the valley floor. When the Forty-Niners headed for California, they were attracted to the goldfields of the Sierra Nevada, which brought them to the place of hardships that they named Death Valley.

Not only gold but borax--the white powder found

National Park Service — SAND DUNES NEAR STOVEPIPE WELLS

near hot mineral springs or volcanic eruptions--brought miners to the region. To haul the huge borax loads from the mines to the railroad, the men hitched up 20-mule teams, which became the trademark of the modern-day soap and detergent company.

Another legacy of the mining days is the mysterious Death Valley gold mine. Rumors of such a mine were circulated by Death Valley Scotty, a publicity stunt man who encouraged his friend, Albert M. Johnson, to build a vacation home here in 1922. Both the Johnsons and Scotty lived here, but the castle is now a part of the monument. Death Valley once supported hundreds of mines, and the remnants of them are spread throughout the monument today. These buildings and shafts are unstable and should not be entered.

The traveler to Death Valley will find many overlooks with exquisite views. Heading south from the visitor center, suggested stops are at Zabriskie Point, Twenty Mule Team Canyon, Dantes View, Badwater, and Artist's Drive. Some of these areas--and others throughout the monument--offer hiking or biking trails.

As unlikely as a desert environment might seem, there are five species of pupfish in the Valley, members of the killifish family which once lived in ancient fresh water lakes. Today they inhabit certain warm springs and saline creeks. The Devils Hole species of pupfish is endangered, but the others should be protected, for their greatest threat is man. Bringing predator and competitive fishes into the region, developing the land,

National Park Service   DEATH VALLEY'S BADWATER

diverting the water, using pesticides--all these practices have combined to threaten the pupfish.

A lack of understanding of Death Valley's environment often leads people to see the desert as worthless land. But there is a tremendous diversity of natural wonders that the conscientious traveler must protect. Here are five of the many ways that growing visitation has adversely affected Death Valley.

1. Badwater houses a spring which supports aquatic life. Oftentimes travelers to the spring stray from the established path, or wade in the water. This tramples the salt crust along the spring, creating a threat to the Badwater snail, a species which may soon be declared endangered. *Travelers should stay on marked trails!*

2. The prehistoric people and Indians who once inhabited this area left behind many artifacts and rock art. These are non-renewable resources; what modern visitors take or destroy cannot be replaced. *Leave all artifacts, even the smallest ones, untouched!*

3. Mountain bikes cause erosion on trails and damage the delicate desert environment. Bicycle tracks can take years to disappear, degrading the aesthetic value of this wonderland. *Bikers: stay on roads!*

4. Water is at a premium in Death Valley, and animals such as the desert bighorn will not approach their natural watering holes if humans are present. Attempting to find another source can be very difficult for animals in this environment. *Travelers should carry their own water and stay away from natural sources.*

5. Habitat destruction from ORV's is a serious threat to the desert's ecology. Use of vehicles off established roads is prohibited in the monument. In nearby areas, there are fewer restrictions on ORV's.

National Park Service — A SEQUOIA GROVE

Sequoia & Kings Canyon N.P.

The largest living thing on earth resides in the Giant Forest in Sequoia National Park. This massive member of the plant world is the General Sherman tree, a 275-foot sequoia. Its trunk alone weighs 1,385 tons and its circumference measures 103 feet. The largest branch is seven feet in diameter. Estimated age of the General Sherman is 2,300 to 2,700 years...and growing. Each year its woody mass increases by a figure equivalent to that of a tree one foot in diameter and 50 feet tall.

The General Sherman was named in 1879 by James Wolverton, for the general under whom he had served in the Civil War. Its forest home, located 84 miles west of Fresno, is also fittingly named, for this is the land of Big Trees. Giant Forest is one of about 75 groves of giant sequoias, which are indigenous only to the western slope of the Sierra Nevada, usually growing between 5,000 and 7,000 feet in elevation.

Naturalist John Muir said of the Big Tree that, "barring accidents, it seems to be immortal." Botanists agree. Chemicals in the wood and bark appear to protect these trees from insects and fungi. The sequoia bark, which can range up to two feet thick, helps to protect it from fire. Because they have a shallow root system with no tap root, sequoias are susceptible to toppling from high wind, heavy snow load, and root

National Park Service GIANT SEQUOIAS

failure, but thus far the General Sherman has withstood these threats. And this is not the only big tree at Sequoia National Park; 16 of the world's 35 largest sequoias live here. All but four share the Giant Forest home with the General Sherman.

Nor are big trees the only attractions at Sequoia. The highest mountain in the contiguous United States, Mt. Whitney, rises here some 14,494 feet. Because of its location on the eastern edge of the park, it is visible inside park boundaries only from the high peaks in a remote wilderness area. Another spectacular geologic feature at Sequoia is Moro Rock, a dome-shaped granite monolith, typical of the domes found in the Sierra Nevada.

Set aside in 1890 to protect the Big Trees from exploitation by loggers, and to preserve the watershed for the San Joaquin Valley below, Sequoia became the second national park in the country after Yellowstone. Adjacent to it on the north is Kings Canyon National Park. It, too, is a haven for Big Trees, but its name comes from the spectacular canyon carved by the Kings River. Just west of the park, this canyon reaches a depth of 8,200 feet, from the river's bottom to the peak of Spanish Mountain. This makes it deeper than either the Hells Canyon of the Snake River in Idaho, or the Colorado River's Grand Canyon in Arizona.

The summit peaks of the High Sierra dominate Kings Canyon. Running 400 miles long and 60 to 80 miles wide, the Sierra Nevada covers a greater territory than the Alps in three countries of Europe. In Kings Canyon alone, there are six peaks taller than 14,000 feet.

J.R. Warner — GRAND SENTINEL, KINGS CANYON N.P.

Extending from the west-central border of Sequoia National Park is a northward-reaching finger of parkland. The northern tip of it is called Grant Grove. Originally this was General Grant National Park, established in 1890. In 1940 more land was added, boundaries were changed, and the park was designated Kings Canyon N.P.

Within this portion of the park lives the General Grant, the third largest sequoia by volume of the trunk. Estimated age of this giant is 1,800 to 2,000 years. The 267.4-foot General Grant's largest branch is 4-1/2 ft. in diameter.

Elsewhere in this park stand three of the world's 35 largest sequoias. The two largest remaining sequoia groves in the world are at Redwood Mountain in Kings Canyon and at Giant Forest in Sequoia.

As the moisture-filled air moves in from the ocean, the Sierra Nevada forces it to rise, cooling the air and causing it to drop its moisture in the form of precipitation. Most of the moisture falls above 5,000 feet, where the sequoias grow. On the dry western slopes below this elevation grows chaparral, a group of drought-resistant, extremely flammable shrubs. Fire plays an important role in maintaining the plant communities in these parks, from chaparral to giant sequoias.

Wymond Eckhardt DEVILS POSTPILE

DEVILS POSTPILE

This unique collection of black basalt columns does, indeed, look like a pile of posts, apparently abandoned by the devil some 100,000 years ago. More imaginative minds claim it is the mammoth natural pipe organ of some superhuman musician. This unusual geologic phenomenon is protected within the boundaries of a national monument near the Mammoth Lakes resort. Running through the monument are the coincident John Muir/Pacific Crest Trails and King Creek Trail, as well as a number of shorter walking paths.

Although this is not the only example of columnar-jointed basalt in the world (there are similar formations in Ireland and Scotland), it is one of the finest. The 60-foot columns which make up this geologic wonder are part of an ancient lava flow. Geologists reckon that newly erupted lava was trapped in a lake formed by a natural dam in the valley of the Middle Fork of the San Joaquin River. This lake may have been 400 feet deep, and probably filled the entire valley. The trapped lava cooled more slowly in shallower parts of the flow, solidifying down from the top and up from the bottom. Shrinkage cracks emanating from the top and bottom created the columnar effect.

This columnar jointing of lava does not often occur in such perfect examples. While most of the pieces at the Postpile are hexagonal (6-sided), as is typical with cracks in lava, there are some examples here that are

Wymond Eckhardt   RAINBOW FALLS

3-, 4-, 5-, and 7-sided as well. Irregularities in cooling probably created these less common shapes. Subsequent years of glacial activity in the park created a smooth, striated, polished surface on the top of the Postpile, giving it the effect of a tiled floor.

The effects of another fascinating geologic occurrence can be seen at Rainbow Falls, where water from the Middle Fork of the San Joaquin River cascades 101 feet over crude columns of a lighter gray basalt. Scientists say the river once flowed about 1,500 feet west of its present course, where it cut a cliff in the rhyodacite on the eastern bank. The river subsequently shifted course for a stretch, creating a new channel for a short distance, and then rejoined its previous route, dropping to the level of its old channel over Rainbow Falls.

There are also mineral springs in the area, indicative of recent volcanic activity. At Soda Springs, iron present in the water oxidizes when it contacts air, giving the river rock a reddish brown color.

In an effort to minimize damage to the environment, a shuttle bus service now runs between Devils Postpile, Agnew Meadows, and Reds Meadow Resort. The bus leaves from the Mammoth Mountain Ski Area and makes stops at 10 locations. There is no charge.

National Park Service — CATHEDRAL ROCKS AT SUNSET

YOSEMITE NATIONAL PARK

The spectacular geology and great climbing opportunities of Yosemite National Park have their roots in the origin of the Sierra Nevada range. This entire region was, about 500 million years ago, covered by a great sea bordered by ancient mountains. As the mountains eroded, the sediment collected at the bottom of the sea and hardened into rock. Uplifting of the earth's crust pushed the rock layers into a NW/SE mountain range. Molten rock formed beneath the mountains as they rose, creating the granite that would become the Sierra Nevada.

As the uplift continued, the western slopes of the mountains became much steeper, giving the streams greater carving force. Sharp, deep canyons appeared where rolling hills had once lain. Still the uplift persisted, forming a fault-block range of mountains with a steep eastern escarpment. The great ice age followed, during which glaciers formed in the high mountains and ground their way downward, scraping the canyons until they became U-shaped instead of V-shaped. This glacier action occurred at least three times, cutting off parts of transitory streams to create cascades and waterfalls.

It was during this period that the Yosemite domes were created. Geologically speaking, domes such as Sentinel, Half Dome, and the Starr Kings were formed

Nat. Park Ser.   UPPER AND LOWER YOSEMITE FALLS

by exfoliation--the peeling away of outer layers of rock on granite that has expanded and formed fracture planes parallel to the surface. Certain other domes, such as Lembert, Fairview, and Liberty Cap, were created when ice covered over the exfoliating granite. Many of these domes are located in the the park's spectacular Yosemite Valley, "The Incomparable Valley" it is often called. The famous Half Dome (8842 ft.) and Sentinel Dome (8122 ft.) are among the best known. At west end of the Valley is the incomparable El Capitan, 7569 feet above sea level at its summit, with a sheer 3,000-foot face.

In addition to the domes, this glacier-carved canyon is home to giant waterfalls, steep cliffs, and huge monoliths contrasted against a flat valley floor. The nation's highest waterfall, Yosemite Falls, is here. The falls--which include Upper, Middle, and Lower---drop a combined distance of 2,425 feet, nearly a half mile! These natural wonders are near the Valley Visitor Center in the south-central portion of the park.

Also on the Valley rim is Glacier Point, offering perhaps the finest views in the park, among them a sheer cliff dropping 3,200 feet straight down. This a popular destination for cross-country skiers, for during the winter the road to Glacier Point is closed beyond the Badger Pass Ski Area.

South of Yosemite Valley, some 35 miles by car, is the Mariposa Grove, largest of the park's three sequoia

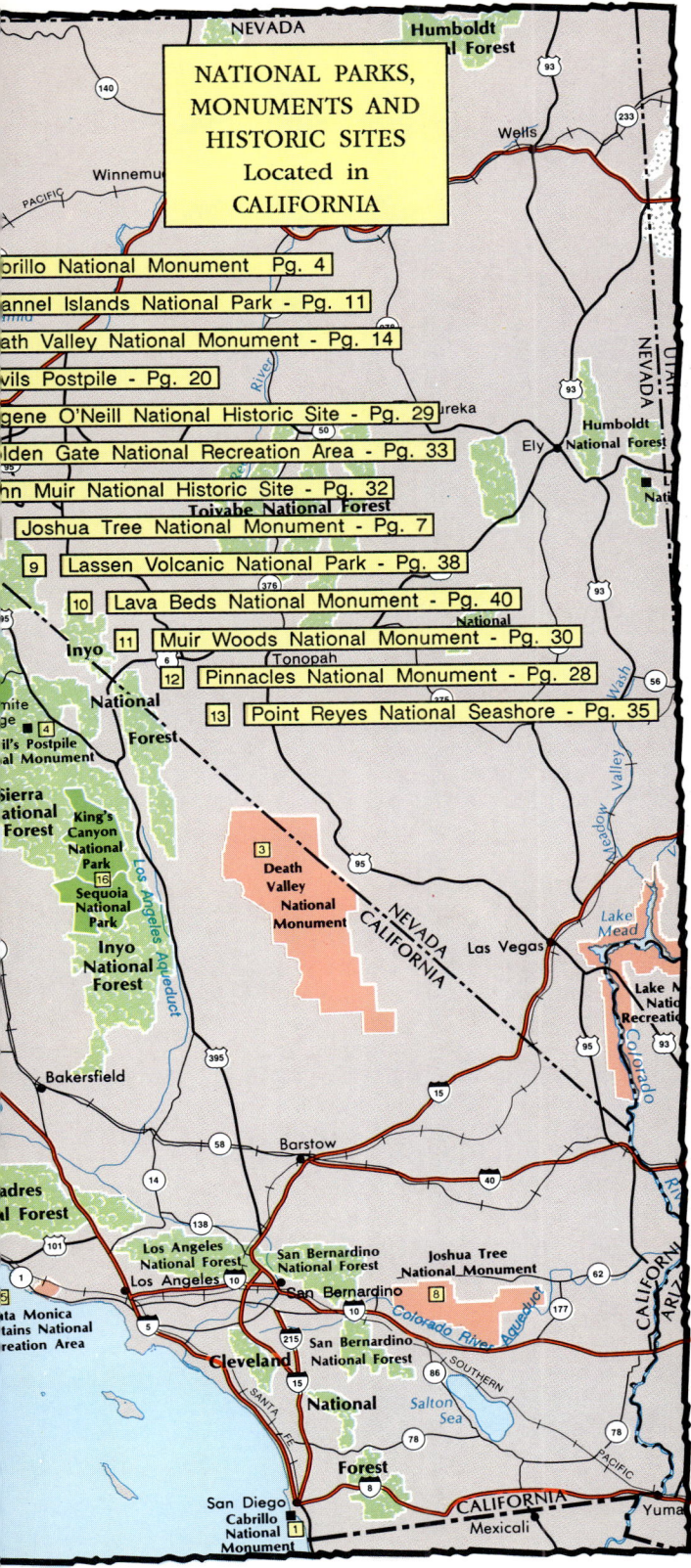

National Park Service — HALF DOME, MERCED RIVER

groves. These great trees, noted for being amazingly fire-resistant (see p.17), are earth's largest living things and also among the oldest. The Grove's Grizzly Giant, 2,700 years old, may be the eldest of all sequoias.

Mariposa Grove is near the park's south entrance. The next stop to the north is Wawona and the Pioneer Yosemite History Center. The Center features historic buildings moved here from other sites and a collection of horse-drawn carriages. This part of the park concentrates on Yosemite's social history. The word Wawona means "Big Tree," and at one time this was an Indian settlement. A hostel was built here in 1856, for this was a good stopping point on the trip from Yosemite Valley to Mariposa. When, in 1875, the Wawona road was opened, the Wawona Hotel also opened and is still being operated today.

The northern third of Yosemite is uncut by roads. Running east to west across this section is the Grand Canyon of the Tuolumne River. On the eastern end is Tuolumne Meadows, the largest subalpine meadow in the Sierra. This popular gathering spot for backpacking expeditions is a region of absolutely spectacular views. It is crossed by the Tioga Road, designed originally as a mining route in 1882-83. Tioga Pass, the highest (9,945 ft.) auto pass in the state, also crosses the crest of the Sierra in this part of the park. About 10 miles (as the crow flies) southeast of Tuolumne Meadows, on Yosemite's eastern border, is Mt. Lyell, the highest peak in the park, at 13,114 ft.

Nat. Park Ser.   (L to R) EL CAPITAN, HALF DOME, BRIDALVEIL FALL

Two of the nation's most scenic long-distance hiking trails pass through parts of Yosemite. The coincident Pacific Crest Trail and John Muir Trail enter the park in the southeast and extend down the Lyell Canyon. At Tuolumne Meadows, the trails divide, the John Muir heading southwest to Yosemite Valley and the Pacific Crest continuing into the northern wilderness of the park to exit near Dorothy Lake. The John Muir Trail was named for the great naturalist who was largely responsible for the establishment of Yosemite National Park.

One of many environmental restoration projects is the revitalizing of Yosemite Valley's meadows and oak woodlands. Stands of pure California black oaks have declined drastically since 1900, due to encroachment by ponderosa pines and incense-cedars, as well as by human impact. Native Ahwahneechee Indians once managed the groves, setting fires annually on the valley floor to clear undergrowth and allow the black oak to flourish. But in the last 100 years, the meadow habitat alone has been reduced from 750 to about 300 acres. The National Park Service have fenced some areas, tilled the soil, and planted native vegetation. Interpretive signs help travelers understand and help the effort.

Another way to help protect the Yosemite environment is to respect the park's large black bear population. "The need to kill bears," rangers remind travelers, "is the result of unmindful people; the bears are not to blame." Getting a nose for human food and garbage can make a bear destructive and dangerous, which may mean it has to be killed. A park brochure warns travelers: YOUR CARELESSNESS WITH FOOD = DEAD BEARS.

PINNACLES NATIONAL MONUMENT

Pinnacles Nat. Mon.

All around, the land is rolling hills, accented with dense stands of Coast Range Chaparral. But rising sharply out of this landscape are the Pinnacles for which the monument was named. The spires serve as a reminder of an ancient volcano which was once active. In its wake, the volcano left the rocky crags which are today the main attraction at this national monument.

The spire-like rock formations, rising from 500 to 1,200 feet, are the work of the San Andreas Rift Zone, a collection of faults just east of the park. Here two tectonic plates come together and the earth's crust is broken, making it vulnerable to earthquake and volcanic action. The Pinnacles were formed some 23 million years ago when molten rock spewed over the land. Frequent eruptions resulted in the formation of a volcanic cone, at one point nearly a mile higher than the park's highest peak today. But as the cone was being formed, the plate on which it was located began moving, ultimately depositing the volcano in its present location--about 195 miles from its original home.

Pinnacles offers challenging technical climbs, plus 26 miles of gentler trails and two sets of talus caves. Summer and fall are very hot and dry, which helps explain the abundance of chaparral. This close growth of brushy, low evergreen shrubs is dependent on hot, quick fires to open its seeds so germination can occur.

National Park Service   O'NEILL'S STUDY AT TAO HOUSE

EUGENE O'NEILL N.H.S.

America's greatest playwright created his masterworks at the beloved Danville home he called his "final harbor." The migratory Eugene O'Neill hoped that Tao House (Chinese for "The Way") would be his last home. It was at Tao that O'Neill wrote the autobiographical plays that would make him most famous. *The Iceman Cometh, Hughie, A Moon For the Misbegotten*, and *A Long Day's Journey Into Night* marked what some critics call the highest achievements of the English-speaking theatre.

For much of his life, O'Neill was a wanderer. His infancy was spent in hotel rooms and in the wings of theaters where his father was acting. In an effort to escape his unstable childhood, young Eugene sailed on various voyages to Honduras, to South America, to England. He became an alcoholic, attempted suicide, and developed TB.

While in a sanitarium for his health, he began to write plays, ultimately winning four Pulitzers and the 1936 Nobel Prize in Literature. Upon moving to California in 1936, he began work on a massive cycle of 11 historical plays. His wife, Carlotta, spent her days decorating Tao House in the style of her passion, Oriental art, and in keeping people away when "The Master" was at work. Ultimately O'Neill's health prohibited him from finishing the play cycle and he was forced to move from his beloved Tao House. Silenced by his illness, he died in a hotel room in Boston in 1953.

Muir Woods Nat. Mon.   REDWOOD CREEK

MUIR WOODS NAT. MON.

Some of the tallest living things in the world are redwood trees, of which there are three well-known species: dawn redwoods found in China; giant sequoias, native to the western slope of the Sierra Nevada; and coast redwoods. This last group lives along a 500-mile strip of the Pacific coast between southern Oregon and Monterey. Although coast redwoods have been extensively logged over the years, many are now under protection at state and national parks, among them Muir Woods National Monument near Mill Valley.

This monument was named for the well-known conservationist by Congressman William Kent and his wife Elizabeth. Because it was so hard to reach, an area of forest along Redwood Creek had been spared from the extensive logging so typical elsewhere along the coast. In 1905, the Kents purchased 295 acres of this old-growth redwood in the hope of protecting the species. They then donated the land to the federal government and subsequently it was made a national monument. Although President Theodore Roosevelt suggested the park be named for its benefactors, the Kents preferred to call it Muir Woods.

Although it is located just 12 miles north of the Golden Gate Bridge, Muir Woods is accessed by steep, winding roads. The monument, which contains six miles of walking trails, is part of the larger Golden

Muir Woods Nat. Mon.   CATHEDRAL GROVE

Gate National Recreation Area. Animal life is not as extensive here as you might imagine in a large wooded area. The redwood forest provides such heavy shade that plant life, and hence the food supply of many animals, is limited. Ferns are common, as are moss and lichen, and mushroom growth. Much of the canyon floor is covered with redwood sorrel.

Although coast redwoods are the dominant tree in the monument, Douglas fir, big-leaf maple, tanbark oak, and bay-laurel also grow here. "This is the best tree-lover's monument that could possibly be found in all the forests of the world," said the conservationist for whom the park was named. "You have done me a great honor and I am proud of it," he told William Kent. Today, more than 1.5 million people visit Muir Woods annually.

Although redwood trees are tough, the forest environment is fragile. In an effort to protect this wilderness habitat, the monument offers no facilities for picnicking or camping, and does not permit pets or radios. Bicycles and horses are allowed only on fire roads. Travelers committed to preserving Muir Woods should also remember not to throw coins in the creek as they are highly toxic to aquatic life. Likewise, visitors should not attempt to tame wildlife by feeding or petting. These are wild animals who need to maintain their own foraging skills and should not become dependent on human handouts.

Russ Finley, N.P.S. JOHN MUIR HOUSE & GROUNDS

JOHN MUIR N.H.S.

Scottish-born naturalist John Muir held, as one of his basic beliefs, that all life forms are important and have a right to exist, humans being no greater or less than other forms of life in this regard. Using this as his base, "John of the Mountains" hiked thousands of miles through the 19th century wilderness of America's west and midwest.

Muir emigrated to Wisconsin with his family in 1848, when he was 10 years old. After a time at the University of Wisconsin, he abandoned his studies in favor of what he called "The University of the Wilderness." His purpose was to save the wilderness at a time when environmental concerns were all but obscured by business and industry's haste to push back the frontier. Wild lands, argued Muir, had a value apart from their usefulness to man, and as such should be preserved.

From the study of his home in Martinez, Muir wrote many influential books and national magazine articles which brought environmental concerns to public notice. He was instrumental in establishing Sequoia and Yosemite National Parks, and was the first to correctly identify glaciers as the creators of Yosemite Valley. Today his home and part of the fruit ranch where he lived from 1890 until his death in 1914 are preserved as a national historic site.

National Park Service MARIN HEADLANDS, GGNRA

GOLDEN GATE N.R.A.

The purpose of the GGNRA is to provide a park in a setting where people are most apt to use it. The Bay Area offers the largest national park in an urban setting in the world. In the midst of 5.5-million people, residents and travelers can still find spectacular wilderness scenery, from woods to ocean. The park also presents a unique cross-section of history, from Spanish to Asian settlement. Access is easy via car, bus, or municipal railway systems.

The GGNRA was set aside in 1972, in an effort to preserve some open space for the enjoyment of the Bay Area's burgeoning population. Its location makes it the most heavily visited of the U.S. national parks; nearly 20 million people travel here each year.

Focal point of the park system is San Francisco's Golden Gate Bridge which spans the Golden Gate and connects Marin County with the San Francisco peninsula. For many years this was the longest span bridge in the world. The park covers both shores. Along the coast are 11 ocean and bay beaches, one of them being among the top four boardsailing areas in the world. Two-thirds of San Francisco's shoreline is part of the GGNRA's public land, making it the largest urban shoreline in the country--some 28 miles. On the cliffs and sand dunes above the ocean, hang gliders fly in what is called _the_ West Coast hang gliding area.

National Park Service THE GOLDEN GATE

The eastern end of the park is home of the National Maritime Museum and Aquatic Park, now part of the San Francisco Maritime N.H.P. Nearby is ever-popular Fisherman's Wharf, where the ferry to Alcatraz Island docks. Travelers can take a 15-minute boat ride, tour the prison, and see the island's pelican roost.

Moving west past Fort Mason--once a port of embarkation--travelers come to Fort Point. The narrow entrance San Francisco harbor is the southern terminus of the Golden Gate Bridge, where a Spanish fort once stood. West of Fort Point and the Presidio of San Francisco, the shoreline leads to Lands End. The Coastal Trail takes hikers along a natural, unspoiled route to this northwesterly point on South Bay. There are more than 100 miles of trails in the GGNRA; in fact, 10 percent of the 400-mile Bay Area Ridge Trail traverses the park. Cliff House, just below Lands End, offers some of the nicest ocean panoramas in the entire park. A beautiful four-mile walk south along the beach brings travelers Fort Funston, a popular hang gliding and picnic spot. Nearby is the San Francisco Zoo.

In the northern section of the park, across the Golden Gate, is Muir Woods, also a part of GGNRA, with its spectacular stand of coast redwoods (see p. 30). The Woods, along with the Marin Headlands, Tennessee Valley, Mount Tamalpais, and the Olema Valley, offer excellent hiking in areas remote from urban sounds. There are two nice beaches here, Muir and Stinson, and a ferry from San Francisco or Tiburon takes travelers to nearby Angel Island.

National Park Service   DRAKES BAY

POINT REYES NAT. SEASHORE

Point Reyes, one of 10 National Seashores in the country, offers some of the most spectacular coastal views--and some of the most treacherous surfs--in America. The beauty of this area is tempered in spots by the danger of tremendously powerful waves and rip currents. The rule of thumb at Great Beach, which includes Point Reyes Beaches (North and South), McClures, and Kehoe Beaches, is this: picnic, beachcomb, hike and bike, enjoy--but don't go near the water! The entire area is subject to severe undertow.

Tucked into Drakes Bay, around the Point to the east and north, the beaches are a little more hospitable. But here, where steep cliffs descend sharply to meet the ocean, another precaution must be kept in mind. The cliffs are very unstable and may crumble without warning. Travelers should not climb on them nor walk near their edges.

Marine wildlife abounds at Point Reyes. Among the more interesting year-round residents are harbor seals, which can be identified by their dark and light spotted coats and their lack of external ear flaps. Point Reyes is a popular "hauling out spot" for these creatures, for they get too cold if they stay in the ocean water all the time. They come ashore to soak up solar heat and to give birth to their pups. Travelers to Point Reyes should be extremely careful not to disturb harbor seals.

DIVIDE MEADOW

It is not uncommon to see a baby seal on the beach, seemingly alone, but it should be left alone. Its mother is probably feeding nearby and will return, but if she finds her babe has been moved, she will likely abandon him. Too much harassment or human interaction causes harbor seals to abandon an area completely.

Point Reyes is also a prime whale watching area. The gray whale migration passes the Point in December and January, headed for the warmer waters of Baja. The grays travel about 5 m.p.h. and surface regularly. From mid-March to May, they pass this way again, on their northern trek to the Bering Sea. In the Drakes Bay area of the shore, grays have been spotted "spy hopping"--sticking their heads out of the water to have a look around. The headlands of Point Reyes offer the best whale watching locations, from Sea Lion Overlook to Chimney Rock, or at the Point Reyes Lighthouse.

The Lighthouse is another fascinating feature of the Seashore. Built in 1870, it stayed in service for 105 years, warning mariners of the heavy winds, fog, and the Point Reyes Headlands which stick out into the sea 10 miles. For here is the second foggiest place in North America and the windiest spot on the Pacific Coast.

In the first 60 years of the lighthouse's existence, there were 46 shipwrecks. This obvious hazard resulted in the establishment of a lifesaving station on the Great Beach in 1888. Rescue crews patrolled the beaches in four-hour shifts, ready to help those who had been caught in an undertow offshore. But the hazards of the

POINT REYES LIGHTHOUSE

first beach site prompted the service to move to a location on Drakes Bay in 1912. The boathouse was upgraded in 1927, and stands today, preserved and protected by the Park Service.

But Point Reyes is more than just ocean and seashore. Forested areas with hiking trails abound. The Olema Valley area to the north and east is administered by Point Reyes. Along its southern edge runs the San Andreas Fault Zone, the backbone of California's earthquake country. A curious fact of geology is that the coastal rocks of Point Reyes match those of the Tehachapi Mountains, more than 300 miles south. This is because the Point Reyes peninsula sits on the Pacific plate, one of the world's six major tectonic plates. The Pacific moves faster than its immediate eastern neighbor, the North American plate, carrying its contents northward at the rate of three inches per year.

Park headquarters are at Bear Valley in the north central area. From here, travelers can take a variety of short hikes, among them the Earthquake Trail, a 0.7-mile walk along the San Andreas Fault. Heading west from the center, travelers come to Tomales Bay State Park, the northernmost section of the peninsula, which moved nearly 20 feet north during the Earthquake of 1906. Further west toward McClures beach is the Tule Elk Range. In the first half of the 19th century, thousands of Tule elk lived here. Not long ago, a herd was returned, and is protected by the sanctuary.

National Park Service — LASSEN PEAK AND DEVASTATED AREA

Lassen Volcanic Nat. Park

The world's largest plug dome volcano began its last series of eruptions in May 1914. More explosions began on May 19, 1915, when molten lava poured 1000 feet down the mountain, melting snow and creating mud flows. By May 22, the blast of fiery gases had destroyed hundreds of trees, but the eruptions continued for another six years.

Lassen Peak retained its record as the most recently erupting volcano in the contiguous 48 states until Mount St. Helens superseded it in 1980. In studying the effects of the Mt. St. Helens eruption and trying to predict the landscape's recovery time and patterns, Lassen served as a valuable laboratory for geologists and environmental experts.

Travelers can study the effects of a volcano's force at The Devastated Area and The Chaos Jumbles. The former was denuded by such volcanic activity as mud flows and gas blasts, while Chaos Jumbles was denuded by a rockfall avalanche. This destruction may have been caused when a huge mass of air was trapped and compressed by rapidly falling lava. With the air acting as a lubricant, the lava picked up speed, to roar through the valley at nearly 100 m.p.h.

Lassen is located on the Pacific Ring of Fire--the unstable region of the earth that encircles the Pacific Ocean and is highly vulnerable to volcanic and earthquake activity. It is the southernmost volcano in the Cascade Range which runs north into Oregon.

National Park Service BUMPASS HELL (FUMAROLE)

Lassen Peak's story goes back some 500,000 years, when the ancient volcano Mount Tehama began its periodic eruptions. What is today the Peak was once a vent on the northern edge of larger Mount Tahama. The main vent on the ancient volcano may have been what is now the Sulphur Works, in the southwestern portion of the park. Several peaks surround the area, which, if they were encircled by a line, would give an idea of the size of ancient Mount Tehama.

Sulphur Works is only one of several geothermal areas at Lassen. There are fumaroles, bubbling mud pots, and boiling-point-temperature springs within the park, some of which are getting hotter. This leads scientists to speculate that either Lassen Peak or Mount Shasta will be the site of the next volcanic eruption in the Cascades.

Lassen Peak, named for explorer Peter Lassen who led gold rush settlers into this area, suffers like many of our national parks, from overuse. Two particularly vulnerable areas are Lassen Peak Trail and the Bumpass Hell Trail. Short-cutting of switchbacks on the trails has carved severe gullies. At Bumpass Hell, too many travelers leave the specially constructed boardwalks to walk on fragile areas, seriously endangering themselves and the natural resource. A severe problem-- here and in other wild areas--is elimination of natural fire. Controlled natural fires should be allowed to burn, for they clean up undergrowth, allowing native vegetation to thrive and reducing the threat of a major fire caused by an oversupply of fuel.

Lava Beds National Monument — SCHONCHIN LAVA FLOW

LAVA BEDS NAT. MON.

A natural fortress created by this area's rugged volcanic rock landscape provided the Modoc Indians with an excellent refuge from the white man during the Modoc War of 1872-73. The Lava Beds region had been the Modoc's home for several thousand years. Here they hunted, fished, and made boats from the tules that grew wild. Then came the white man, and ultimately a demand by the United States government for the Modocs to move from their homeland onto a reservation where they were to live with other natives who had been their lifelong enemies. The experiment was a disaster, and the Modocs pleaded for a home by themselves back in their native Lava Beds region.

Frustrated and unhappy, more and more Indians began escaping. Finally, on November 29, 1872, the army sent out men to round up and bring back the natives. In the fighting that followed, a group of 120-130 natives escaped to the lava beds. For nearly half a year, they were able to repel some 1000 soldiers. When at last they could hold out no longer, their leader, Captain Jack, surrendered. He and his leaders were hanged, and the rest of the natives banished to a reservation in Oklahoma.

This rugged landscape that served as a haven for the Modocs is the result of millions of years of volcanic activity. Northern California has a long history of

Lava Beds National Monument — SCHONCHIN BUTTE

volcanism which continues into modern times. The many eruptions in the Lava Beds area have left cinder cones, shield volcanoes, lava tubes, spatter cones, chimneys, and other evidence. Nearly 200 caves can be found here, several of them near the Visitor Center along a route called Cave Loop Road. Mushpot Cave, which leads off the visitor center, is accessible to the public and has lights installed.

These caves are much different than a traditional limestone cave. When 1800-degree lava comes spewing from a volcano, the surface and edges cool quickly, but beneath them the lava continues to flow, like a stream that is frozen on top continues to run beneath. When the flow stops, an empty tube called a lava tube is left inside the hardened crust. Much of the lava erupted from Mammoth Crater near the southern edge of the park, created nearly 30,000 years ago. When, on occasion, the roof of a lava tube collapses, an ecosystem may develop inside, as plants and animals take it over as a home.

Travelers to Lava Beds can also climb any of several large cinder cones in the monument, such as the 3/4-mile trail up Schonchin Butte. But these formations erode very easily, so hikers must not stray from marked paths. Spatter cones--created when globs of molten lava accumulate atop each other-- are of interest to photographers, for they offer a nice array of natural color. Two of them--Fleener Chimneys and Black Crater--are almost castle-like in appearance.

Greg Gnesios WHISKEYTOWN LAKE

WHISKEYTOWN-SHASTA-TRINITY

The Whiskeytown Unit, administered by the National Park Service, is one of 18 National Recreation Areas in the country. But Whiskeytown is only one section of this NRA. The other two, Shasta and Trinity units, are managed by the U.S. Forest Service. Their common purpose is the same, however--to offer northern California travelers the ultimate outdoor experience in a setting of spectacular man-made reservoirs surrounded by beautiful mountains.

Water skiing, boating, fishing, canoeing, scuba diving, swimming--all are available at the area's three impounded lakes, Shasta, Whiskeytown, and Lewiston, in addition to Clair Engle Lake in the northern section of the Trinity unit. In addition, travelers can enjoy camping, horseback riding, hunting, hiking, and even gold panning. In fact, Whiskeytown has its heritage in the gold rush days. It was settled in 1849 when gold was discovered nearby at Reading's Bar. Before the townsite was flooded by the building of the Whiskeytown Dam in 1963, the cemetery and local store were moved for preservation. They can be visited today by traveling south from the Whiskeytown Dam.

To the southeast, and just outside park boundaries, is Old Shasta, a state historic park administered by the state. Shasta was a prosperous gold mining center that

Greg Gnesios BOATING AT WHISKEYTOWN

once boarded as many as 100 freight teams per night. At its peak, the town produced $100,000 worth of gold per month, and miners were known to have moved their cabins to follow illusive veins of gold beneath them. In the far northwest section of the Whiskeytown unit is Tower House Historic District, another area of interest from the gold rush era.

Mines have dotted the area for more than a century, and the mining operations have left intact little of archaeological or historical value. Settlement by Native Americans goes back 1000+ years. When the white man arrived in the area, it was inhabited by the Wintu, a people very respectful and protecting of their environment. In the late 19th-century the Wintu, like other tribes in the region, suffered from encroachment by the white man. But the Wintu maintain viable cultural ties to the present.

Today, park rangers encourage travelers to be as sensitive to the environment as were the Wintu. This means protecting nesting sites of the endangered bald eagle, America's national bird. Travelers are also asked to discourage the black bear problem by storing food or garbage in vehicles.

Vandalism, reports a park administrator, "is rampant in Whiskeytown." Travelers are encouraged to report destruction to park property through the "Park Watch" program. A more positive approach, for children, is to participate in Whiskeytown's Junior Ranger program, which teaches environmental ethics and natural resource conservation. Water conservation is also urged, since the state has, for six years, been plagued by drought.

Redwood N.P.   DWARFED BY A COAST REDWOOD

REDWOOD NATIONAL PARK

This national park was established to protect the large stands of coast redwoods which populate northern California. These amazing trees grow only in a small strip of land from southern Oregon to Monterey, no farther than 30 miles inland, and at elevations below 3,000 feet. They thrive in the cool moist climate of California's north coast region. Not only is the climate conducive to their growth; the abundance of fog along the coast helps protect these redwoods from water loss through evaporation. In fact, say botanists, fog plays a greater role in the redwood's life than does the high annual rainfall in this region.

Coast redwoods are taller than any other trees in the world. Their relatives, the giant sequoias, are greater in diameter and mass, but the redwoods outstrip them in height. The Wilt Chamberlain of the forest lives in Tall Trees Grove along Redwood Creek and stretches to 367.8 feet. For its height, the redwood takes up a relatively small surface area. This feature gives it the distinction of having the greatest volume of living matter per unit of surface area of any creature in the plant kingdom.

These unique trees have been known to live 2000 years, presumably because there are no known diseases or insects which can kill them. What does endanger them is fire, but even this is more destructive to young

Redwood N.P.   REDWOOD'S COASTLINE

trees. The oldsters have bark up to a foot thick which protects them. Wind can also cause problems, because the trees have quite a shallow root system for their height. Roots extend only 10 to 13 feet deep, covering an area 60 to 80 feet wide.

Another threat to the coast redwood has been man. Northern California is big timber country, and logging interests have long battled naturalists for rights to the trees. It took nearly 90 years for environmentalists to win protection for a small strip of trees along Redwood Creek. No sooner had Congress granted national park status to this area than the push began to expand it. But by the time Sierra Club and Save-the-Redwoods supporters were victorious, ten years later, much of the annexed area had been heavy and devastatingly logged.

Today's travelers to the park should continue to protect this great natural legacy. *Don't damage the world's tallest living thing!* Incredible as it seems, many visitors have left with a piece of the giant's bark in their pockets. Park personnel don't want to fence the tree, but travelers must act responsibly or the access will be restricted.

Don't disturb marine life in the tidepools. Redwood National Park's long expanse of coastline offers great opportunities for tidepooling. But again, travelers must observe these interesting creatures in a responsible manner. Please don't touch; they are protected by California law.

National Park Service   YOSEMITE'S VERNAL FALL

Our Endangered Parks

Soon we may have to add to the list of endangered species, America's national parks and monuments. In what it termed "a wake-up call to the American public," the National Parks and Conservation Assoc. (a non-profit, non-government organization) listed five "crucial threats" to America's parklands.

One of those was "impact of increased visitation." By the year 2000, the National Park Service expects 360 million travelers a year to its lands. But this news is bittersweet. While it's nice that so many of us can enjoy America's parklands, our large numbers put a tremendous strain on natural and human resources. The Park Service is already operating on a tight budget and cannot afford to hire the number of rangers it needs to monitor this increased visitation. The NPCA estimates that 1200 additional rangers are needed to supplement the 3200 currently on staff.

Much controversy surrounds the pressure on America's national parks. One side claims that an annual budget of $900-million is not enough for the Park Service to accomplish its 1916 mandate of preserving the parks "unimpaired for the enjoyment of future generations." Critics say the budget isn't the culprit; it's management and administration of the budget.

In the meantime, the parks continue to suffer.

National Park Service   JOSHUA TREE NAT. MON.

Although there's little the average traveler can do to solve administrative or budget problems, there are many ways that each of us--all 360 million of us--can work to protect this heritage. Above all we need to remember that national parks are not theme parks. Most are unique biological reserves. It is the responsibility of each visitor to respect and protect the wildlife and botanic life, the cultural and historical artifacts that we come here to see. *Most of these are non-renewable resources!*

Common sense on the part of travelers can reverse the threat of deterioration of our parks. Here are just a few suggestions for park traveler etiquette:

* Use public transportation, foot or horseback access whenever possible, in an effort to reduce environmental pollution.

* Stay on marked trails and roads to help prevent soil erosion and subsequent loss of plant life.

* Take nothing out except what you brought in. Preserve what you see for the next visitor.

* Watch but do not interact with wildlife. A seemingly tame animal can display its wild state without warning. Tempting or feeding wildlife also reduces animals' self-reliance. Who will feed them when you're not there?

* Consider it a privilege, not a right, to be able to visit these lands. And treat them as you would your own sacred piece of property for future preservation.

Greg Gnesios   WHISKEYTOWN LAKE

NAMES & NUMBERS

Cabrillo Nat. Mon.
PO Box 6670
San Diego, CA 92166-0670
619-557-5450

Channel Islands Nat. Park
1901 Spinnaker Drive
Ventura, CA 93001
805-658-5730

Devils Postpile Nat. Mon.
PO Box 501
Mammoth Lakes, CA 93546
619-934-2289
Closed in winter.

Death Valley Nat. Mon.
Death Valley, CA 92328
619-786-2331

Eugene O'Neill NHS
PO Box 280
Danville, CA 94526
510-838-0249

Golden Gate Nat. Rec. Area
Fort Mason
San Francisco, CA 94123
415-556-4484

John Muir NHS
4202 Alhambra Ave.
Martinez, CA 94553
510-228-8860

Joshua Tree Nat. Mon.
74485 National Monument Dr.
Twentynine Palms, CA 92277-3597
619-367-7511

Lassen Volcanic Nat. Park
PO Box 100
Mineral, CA 96063-0100
916-595-4444

Lava Beds Nat. Mon.
PO Box 867
Tulelake, CA 96134
916-667-2282

Muir Woods Nat. Mon.
Mill Valley, CA 94941
415-388-2596

Pinnacles Nat. Mon.
Paicines, CA 95043
408-389-4485

Point Reyes Nat. Seashore
Point Reyes, CA 94956
415-663-1092

Redwood Nat. Park
1111 Second Street
Crescent City, CA 95531
707-464-6101

Santa Monica Mts. N.R.A.
30401 Agoura Road - #100
Agoura Hills, CA 91301
602-622-1999

Sequoia & Kings Canyon N.P.
Three Rivers, CA 93271
209-565-3341

Whiskeytown-Shasta-Trinity National Recreation Area
PO Box 188
Whiskeytown, CA 96095-0188
916-241-6584

Yosemite Nat. Park
PO Box 577
Yosemite, CA 95389
209-372-0478